D1370378

K.T. CROWNHILL

THE UNOFFICIAL HARRY POTTER COOKBOOK

Table of Contents

Chapter 1: Apprentice

Chapter 2: Adept

Chapter 3: Archmage

SPREAD THE MAGIC

Did you enjoy this book? Help us spread the word!
It's really easy - write a short (and honest) review on Amazon or any other online bookstore. The more reviews a book has, the more Wizards will stumble upon it.

If you're not sure how to leave a review, visit: artofwizardry.com/review for an easy step-by-step guide.

FREE GOODIES

Awesome stuff. no joke!

The Magic Library stores an exclusive collection of free printables: Acceptance Letters, Social Gathering Invitations and Potion Labels. Get them now at: artofwizardry.com/library

BORING BITS...

HeadTeacher's Introduction

Welcome Wizards one and all.

Cast your eyes and feast on a stupendous book full of magical flavours. Even the brightest of Magicians require memory of epic proportions to prepare these remarkable brews – You take a little bit of this, mix it with a little bit of that, boil and bubble and watch the magic froth to life in front of your very own eyes.

If only it was that easy!

No one knows exactly when each recipe came to be, but we know that each came from a Wizard or a Witch just like you and me. If you work hard, learn what each ingredient does, mix them together all right, then you too will be as the mighty aliment enchanter Professor K.T. Crownhill!

Know your herb, know your spice and make sure the kitchen has no mice. Chop and dice, burn on fire, cool with ice. Lo and behold before your very eyes... a wondrous vice.

Food fit for Wizards all alike!

M.E. Atherton

Professor Marvolo Everett Atherton II (the second)

Headteacher "Art of Wizardry" School of Magic

Foreword from the Author

Cookery occupies such a large place in the history of Magic that to include all the details within the limits of one volume would need the powers of an Archmage no less potent than was he who confined the genie in a bottle.

The recipes both for simple and elaborate dishes given in this book have been thoroughly tested by constant use in my cookery classes at the *"Art of Wizardry"* School of Magic. They were carefully selected and have been pronounced excellent by persons of discriminating taste.

Apprentices who come to our faculty from all over the world often bring the most popular recipes from their respective localities. These formulas, together with those originated by our wizarding ancestors afford an unusual variety for the lover of enchanted cooking.

The essence of the Magical Kitchen

There is a science and there is a magic of cooking.
The science tells what should be done and why; while magic takes hold and does its thing - without, in some cases, knowing the reason why certain spells produce certain results.

The sense of taste can be rebellious. It will cry out against the best appearing dish, if its flavour is not the greatest.
There is but one way to sure success:
the Wizard himself must be a force who casts the spell and invests it with form and aroma of irresistible attractiveness.

This is the true magic of cookery; and privileged is the home where one presides who knows this art, and makes each meal a true feast, and every guest a grateful participant.

The Curriculum Committee of the Faculty of Enchanted Cookery has accepted the following chapters, in order of a degree of skill:

Fairy's note on Nutrition

One must be warned - some of our delicious recipes contained herein *(especially desserts and candies)* are to be enjoyed in moderation.

Overindulging may auto-activate the spell transforming you into a giant sugar puff!

About the Author

K.T. Crownhill is a Professor at the "Art of Wizardry" School of Magic and holds a chair on the Faculty of Enchanted Cookery. She is a certified Witch with over 65 years experience in brewing potions.

Miss Crownhill lives in a tiny hut on Hen's legs, buried somewhere in Masovian forests, together with her seventeen cats and a pet dragon named Jerry.

Apprentice

LEVEL 1 - BEGINNERS
UNDER 8'S
WITH ADULT SUPERVISION

ear Apprentice,

Let our "Magical Kitchen" adventure begin! Start with the basic rules and follow each one carefully.

1. Be Orderly

Do your planning before you begin. Choose a recipe, read it through carefully, understand it clearly. Collect the ingredients it calls for and assemble all necessary tools and utensils.

2. Choose Quality Ingredients

You can't cook a first-rate enchanted dish with second-rate ingredients! Be sure of their freshness & quality.

3. Measure Accurately

The strongest magical spell won't banish mistakes made with incorrectly measured ingredients. To assure uniformly successful results, all recipes mention quantities in both imperial and metric systems.

4. Get Help

Are you a wizard of only a few winters old? Ask an adult magician to aid your efforts.
Nothing contributes more towards deliciousness than a magical alliance with a more experienced cook.

Butterbrew PANCAKES

Time required:
20 min

Servings:
6-8 portions

6

Ingredients

- ★ 1 cup (125g) Self-Raising Flour
- ★ 1 tbsp Sugar
- ★ 1 Egg, lightly beaten
- ★ 3/4 cup (180ml) Whole Milk
- ★ 2 oz (50g or 4 tbsp) Butter, melted

For the sauce

- ★ 3/4 cup (5 oz) Butterscotch Flavoured Chips
- ★ 4 tbsp Cream (double / heavy)
- ★ 1 tbsp Honey
- ★ Pinch of Salt

Method

Mix flour and sugar together in a medium bowl. Beat in the egg. Gradually pour milk in, whisking continually. Batter should become smooth and lump-free.

Place a frying pan over a medium heat. Cover its surface with butter. Pour 1/4 cup (3 tbsp) of batter for each pancake. When large bubbles form, flip the pancake to the other side and fry until golden. Continue until you're out of batter.

For the Butterbrew Sauce -
Place chips, cream, honey and salt in a microwave-safe bowl. Set the microwave on medium setting for 60 seconds. Stir carefully (warning: the bowl can get hot!). If the consistency is still too thick, microwave for another 15 seconds and repeat if necessary. Best served warm over the lovely pancakes.

SAND~WITCH

Time required: 5 min
Servings: 1 portion

INGREDIENTS

* 2 slices Bacon
* 1 English Muffin, *split and toasted*
* 1 tbsp Mayonnaise
* 1 tsp Honey Mustard   * 1 slice Mild Cheese
* 2 slices Tomato   * Pinch of Salt
* 3-4 slices Gherkin   * Black Olives, *as decoration*

METHOD

Fry bacon slices on a frying pan over medium heat until light gold and crispy. Drain excess fat on a paper towel and set aside.

Halve English muffin and toast it. Spread one half with mayonnaise and another with mustard. Lay a tomato and gherkin slices on the bottom half, top with cheese. Shout out 3 times: "Bongusta!".

Season with salt. Top with bacon. Close with second half of the muffin and add "eyes" out of black olives.

SEAWEED WATER

Time required:
7 min + 1 hour

Servings:
11 cups

Perfect for temporary growth of gills!!!

INGREDIENTS

1 CUCUMBER *long, washed, without any wrinkles*

3 FRESH MINT SPRIGS *washed*

1/2 LEMON *juiced*

11 CUPS (2,5 LITRES) WATER *(filtered, mineral, or aloe water)*

METHOD

1. Wash the cucumber properly, cut the stems off. Carefully peel it *vertically,* from one end to the other.

   Note: Don't throw away the skin! One might need it later to decorate the drinks for additional sliminess.

2. Aim to get *long, thin ribbons.* Continue peeling until you get to the seeds. Then stop and move to the opposite side of the cucumber. You can throw away the seeds, or better yet - eat them!

3. Place the sliced cucumber, mint, and juice of ½ lemon in a large jug. Next, pour water into it. Cover and place in the refrigerator for a *minimum of 1 hour.* The longer you infuse it, the stronger the flavour will become.

4. Pour into glasses and serve with slices of cucumber as garnish.

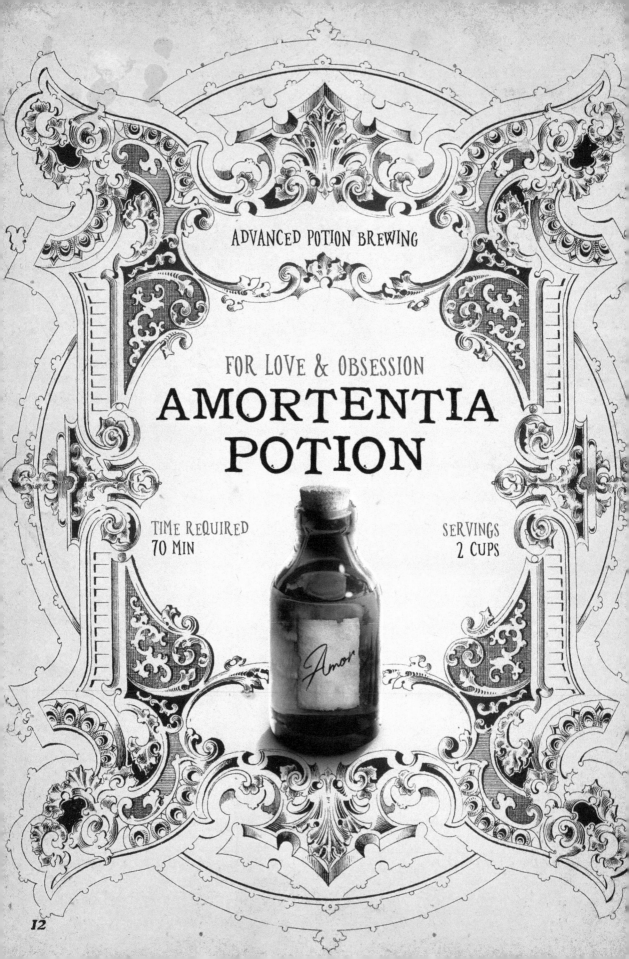

INGREDIENTS

2 CUPS (16 OZ. 500ML) WATER

2 HIBISCUS TEABAGS

2 TSP HONEY

2-3 DROPS VANILLA EXTRACT

1/2 CUP (4 OZ. 120 ML) LEMONADE

METHOD

PUT A KETTLE ON, BOIL THE WATER.
DROP TEABAGS INTO IT AND SHOUT OUT 3 TIMES:
"AMU MIN" WHILE BLINKING YOUR RIGHT EYE.

DISSOLVE THE HONEY AND ADD VANILLA.
STIR AND PUT ASIDE TO COOL FOR 15 MINUTES.

REMOVE THE TEABAGS AND REFRIGERATE
FOR AN HOUR.

TO SERVE, POUR HALF OF THE TEA (8 OZ. 250ML) AND
HALF OF THE LEMONADE (2 OZ. 60ML) INTO A GLASS
AND ADD ICE TO SERVE.

ALTERNATIVELY, POUR THE MIXTURE INTO
INDIVIDUAL VIALS/BOTTLES.

Creamy Pumpkin Smoothie

INGREDIENTS

1 BANANA *medium*

1 CUP (250G) PLAIN YOGURT

1/4 TEASPOON GROUND CINNAMON

1/4 TEASPOON PUMPKIN PIE SPICE
or nutmeg/all spice

2 TABLESPOON HONEY

2/3 CUP (150G) PUMPKIN PURÉE
(fresh or canned)

Time required: **5 min** *Servings:* **1 large or 2 small**

Method

1. ADD ALL THE INGREDIENTS TO THE BLENDER. *(in the order listed)*

2. BLEND UNTIL SMOOTH.

   For thinner texture, add more milk.
   To thicken – add more purée.

3. POUR INTO A GLASS. *(or 2 small glasses)*

4. ADD WHIPPED CREAM AND GRIND CINNAMON ON TOP, IF DESIRED.

BUTTERALE LATTE

rich & warming brew

— original —

T 266.738

II ak.5416

Time required:
3 min

Servings:
2 cups

Ingredients

❖
---

2 CUPS (480ML) MILK *whole (3.2%)*

1 TBSP HONEY

1 TSP BROWN SUGAR

A PINCH OF GROUND CINNAMON

3/4 CUP (180 ML) ESPRESSO
or strong brewed coffee / decaf (hot)

VANILLA SUGAR *to sprinkle on top (optional)*

Method

❖
---

1. *Pour milk into a large jar. Make sure it fits into your microwave.*

2. *Add honey, sugar and cinnamon and close the lid. Shake for 60 seconds. Take the lid off and warm up the milk in the microwave for about 30-45 seconds.*

3. *Divide hot coffee between two cups. Then pour in the milk mixture. If there is any foam left in the jar, spoon it out too.*

4. *Sprinkle with vanilla sugar. Serve while still warm, pair with some butterbrew cookies.*

Acid
POPS

TIME REQUIRED: *3 min* SERVINGS: 6

INGREDIENTS

6 Round Lollipops

3 tbsp Honey

2-3 packs Pop Rocks

METHOD

Remove wrappers from lollipops.

Place honey in a small bowl.

Pour pop rocks into another bowl.
Dip each lollipop in honey and
then dip in pop rocks.

Repeat until you're out of lollies.

Never eat more than ten at a time!

Anno. 1617.

Treacle
FUDGE

TIME REQUIRED:
20 MINUTES

SERVINGS:
24 PIECES

Ingredients

1 CAN (385-400 G) CONDENSED MILK

1/2 CAN (200 G) GOLDEN SYRUP

1 CUP (200 G) SUPERFINE/CASTER SUGAR

1 CUP (2 STICKS, 225G) BUTTER

3 TBSP BREADCRUMBS

1 TSP (5 ML) VINEGAR

1 TSP (5 ML) VANILLA EXTRACT

Method

PLACE CONDENSED MILK, GOLDEN SYRUP, SUGAR AND BUTTER IN A MICROWAVE-SAFE BOWL. DON'T MIX IT TOGETHER. SET THE MICROWAVE ONTO A HIGH SETTING FOR 2 MINUTES.

REMOVE FROM THE MICROWAVE (WARNING: THE BOWL CAN GET HOT!). ADD BREADCRUMBS AND STIR WELL. MICROWAVE ON HIGH AGAIN, STOPPING EVERY 2 MINUTES TO STIR – UNTIL THE FUDGE TURNS GOLDEN BROWN. DO BE CAREFUL, THE BOWL AND THE MIXTURE GETS VERY HOT.

REMOVE FROM THE MICROWAVE, STIR IN THE VANILLA EXTRACT AND VINEGAR.

GREASE A RECTANGULAR DISH, POUR THE FUDGE IN. ALLOW TO COOL FOR A WHILE UNTIL IT FIRMS A BIT, BUT IS NOT SET COMPLETELY. PORTION THE FUDGE INTO EVEN CHUNKS.

SET ASIDE TO COOL. STORE IN A DRY, COOL PLACE.

Headteacher's
PENSiEVE

Time required: 2h 15min   *Servings:* 4-5

Ingredients

1 large box Blue Gelatin / Jelly

Hot Water

1 tsp Icing / Powdered Sugar

1 cup *(240 ml)* Heavy Whipping Cream

Blueberries
optional

Allows reviewing your memories

Method

Step 1

Make gelatin according to package directions
and let set in the fridge for 2 hours.

Once gelatin is set, crush it with a fork into chunks.

Step 2

Place sugar into the mixing bowl, add whipping cream.
Whisk just until the cream reaches stiff peaks.

Step 3

Begin layering the dessert: cover a few spoonfuls of jelly
with a layer whipped cream.

Repeat the process until you're out of ingredients.
Throw in a few blueberries while you're at it.
Serve chilled.

ROCK
CAKE

Crunchy & Fruity

ROCK CAKES

Time required:
25 min

Servings:
12

Ingredients

- 2 CUPS (8 OZ, 225G) SELF RAISING FLOUR
- 1/2 TSP PUMPKIN PIE SPICE OR MIXED SPICE, *optional*
- 1/2 CUP (100G) BUTTER
- 1/3 CUP (75G) CASTER SUGAR
- 5.5 OZ (150G) RAISINS, *or other dried fruit, nuts or chocolate chips*
- 1 MEDIUM EGG

Method

Preheat oven to 400°F (200°C). Sieve flour & spices into a large mixing bowl. Roughly chop butter into chunks. Using your hands, rub the butter pieces into the flour.

Once the texture starts to look like breadcrumbs - stop rubbing!

Add in caster sugar and raisins. Beat the egg in a small bowl and add to the mixture. Mix firmly with a fork until a stiff, almost rock-like consistency is formed.

Line the baking tray with parchment. Using a tablespoon, form 12 rocky heaps. Don't worry about the shapes.
Bake for 10 to 12 minutes until they are firm and golden brown.

Allow to cool before eating. Store in a dry, cool place.

Cockroach
CLUSTERS

Crunchy & Delicious

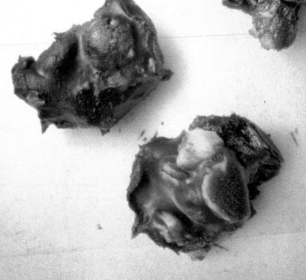

Time required:
1 h 20 min

Servings:
lots & lots

INGREDIENTS

1 cup *approx.125 g* Mixed Nuts & Dried Fruit

5.5 oz *150 g* Milk Chocolate Chips/ Morsels

5.5 oz *150 g* Dark Chocolate Chips/ Morsels

METHOD

Step 1

Chop the selection of nuts & dried fruit into bits,
put them aside.

Step 2

Place the milk & dark chocolate chips into a microwave
safe bowl. Set the microwave at 70% power for 60
seconds, take it out and stir the chocolate well.

Step 3

Microwave again for additional 15 seconds at 70% power.
Then stir until chocolate has completely melted.

Step 4

Now add chopped nuts & dried fruit to the chocolate
bowl, mix it well. Take spoonfuls and drop them onto a
serving plate lined with aluminium foil or even better -
drop them onto a silicone mat.

Step 5

Place in the refrigerator for 20 minutes until the
chocolate sets. Store in a jar - in a dry place.

Time required:
10 min

Servings:
2 cups

Bat's Blood Soup

also known as *Marshmallow Fondue*

INGREDIENTS

* 11 OZ (300 G) DARK CHOCOLATE CHIPS / MORSELS
* 2/3 CUP (160 ML) DOUBLE / HEAVY CREAM
* 2 CUPS (4 OZ, 115G) MINI MARSHMALLOWS
* 1 TSP VANILLA EXTRACT, *to taste*

METHOD

Pour cream and chocolate chips into a medium-sized pan. Cook over low heat, stirring continuously.

Add marshmallows and stir until smooth. Add vanilla extract and blend it into the mass.

Pour over to a cauldron or a fondue pot and serve together with a selection of goods to dip: pieces of fruit, marshmallows and sweets.

Adept

Congratulations my Wizard on mastering the recipes featured in the Apprentice's section.

You have now officially advanced to the Adept level of Enchanted Cookery. Let's take your cooking to new heights and work on more challenging dishes and brews.

Among the contents of this chapter a young Wizard might recognize some recipes which, through their own practical experience and observation, and through their previous study of the subject, have become perfectly familiar to them. If they appear here, it is of course not with a claim for novelty, but for the sake of completeness, and for the benefit of those less well informed.

Every recipe contained herein is a genuine and well-proportioned mixture that contains nothing but what is essential to its perfection.

Before we proceed further, a gentle reminder from our Headteacher - Professor Marvolo Everett Atherton II:

While an Adept is ready to undertake magical activities more independently, adult Wizard's supervision is still highly advisable. Stay safe in the kitchen!

BREAKFAST
COOKIES
WITH BUTTERBREW

Time required:
25 min

Servings:
20 cookies

Ingredients

- ★ 1 cup (2 sticks, 225 g) Butter, softened
- ★ 1 cup (200 g) Sugar
- ★ 1/2 cup (110 g) Dark Brown Sugar
- ★ 1 large Egg
- ★ 2 tsp Vanilla Extract
- ★ 1+2/3 cups (210 g) Self Rising Flour
- ★ 1 tsp Gingerbread Spice (or cinnamon)
- ★ 1/4 tsp Salt
- ★ 1+1/2 cups Instant Oats

Method

Preheat oven to 350ºF (180ºC).

Using an electric mixer, blend together butter with both sugars. The texture will become fluffy. Mix in the egg and vanilla extract.

In a separate bowl, sieve flour and combine with gingerbread spice and salt. Stir into buttery mixture. Add in oats, blending them in gently with a spoon.

Line 2 baking trays with parchment paper. Shape dough into balls (2 tablespoons per each), flatten each one with a spoon.

Place in an oven for 10 minutes until golden. Allow to cool before eating. Store in a dry, cool place.

Time required:
45 min

Servings:
16 rolls

Sausage Rolls

INGREDIENTS

1 CUP (125 G) PLAIN FLOUR
5 TBSP (38 G) COCOA POWDER
1 EGG
1 TBSP BUTTER
2 TSP VANILLA EXTRACT
2-3 TBSP HONEY
PINCH OF SALT

METHOD

Preheat the oven to 350°F (180°C).

Using an electric mixer, blend all ingredients together until the texture becomes doughy.

Line the baking tray with parchment paper. Roll the dough into blueberry-sized balls and place them on the tray.

Bake the puffs for 10-15 minutes, tossing from time to time.

Remove to cool. Store in a dry place.

Can't believe it's not butterbeer...

Butterbrew

2 litre
cream soda

drop both extracts into the soda bottle.

put the cap on & shake gently until combined.

3 Tbsp
butter extract

2 Tsp
rum extract

Creamy Topping

1 cup
whipping cream

200 gram
(7 oz jar)
marshmallow creme / fluff

combine both with a mixer until silky smooth.

POUR THE BUTTERBREW INTO A GLASS & DRIZZLE WITH THE CREAM TOPPING.

Ingredients

12 fl oz (2 litre bottle) Cream Soda
3 tbsp Butter Extract
2 tsp Rum Extract

Creamy Topping

1 cup (240 ml) Whipping Cream
7 oz jar (200 gram) Marshmallow Crème

Optional Toppings: Butterscotch Sauce, Chocolate
Sauce, Chocolate chips, Cinnamon

Method

Step 1 Open the cream soda bottle. Pour both extracts into it and put the cap back on. SLOWLY rotate the bottle until the contents are combined.

Step 2 Beat the whipping cream on high speed using an electric mixer until soft peaks form. Add the marshmallow crème and continue whipping. Stop when a loose whipped cream forms.

Step 3 Pour the butterbeer into a glass and drizzle with the creamy topping. Serve immediately.

Pumpkin Juice

Wizard's Favourite

Time required:
1h 20min

Servings:
5 cups

INGREDIENTS

1 Pumpkin (Sugar or Pie Pumpkin) *4 pounds in weight (1.8kg)* ·
2 cups *480 ml* Apple Juice · 1 cup *240 ml* Peach Nectar ·
1 tsp Pumpkin Pie Spice · 1/2 tsp Almond Extract · 1/3 cup *110 g* Honey ·
Pinch of Salt · Orange Slices, Cinnamon Sticks *for decoration*

METHOD

Step 1 Cut the pumpkin into large chunks. Place them onto a baking tray. Pour some water over the pieces - so that the entire bottom of the tray is covered. Roast in the oven for 30-40 minutes in 350°F (180°C) until soft (check with fork).

Step 2 Remove from oven, wait for the pumpkin to cool. Don't pour the water out, as we will need it later. Carefully remove the skin. Blend the pumpkin pieces together with the water we've kept from before.

Step 3 In a deep cooking pan mix together a cup and a half of the blended pumpkin, as well as the rest of the ingredients. Bring the pan to boil, then reduce the heat. Simmer for 20 minutes stirring occasionally.

Step 4 Chill to serve. Decorate with cinnamon sticks or thin slices of orange.

A 4-pound fresh pumpkin makes around 3-3.5 cups of cooked puree. If you've got too much - just eat it! :)

43

LIQUID LUCK

TIME REQUIRED:
35 MINUTES

SERVINGS:
4 CUPS

INGREDIENTS

* 1/4 CUP (85 G) HONEY
* 1/2 CUP (120 ML) WATER
* 3/4 CUP (19 G) THINLY CHOPPED BASIL LEAVES
* 4 LIMES + SOME FOR GARNISH
* 5 CUPS (1.2 LITRE, 40 OZ) CARBONATED WATER CHILLED

METHOD

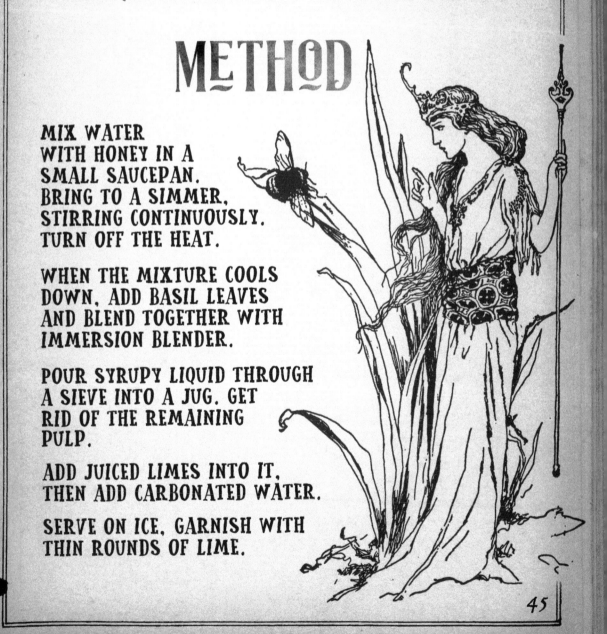

MIX WATER WITH HONEY IN A SMALL SAUCEPAN. BRING TO A SIMMER, STIRRING CONTINUOUSLY. TURN OFF THE HEAT.

WHEN THE MIXTURE COOLS DOWN, ADD BASIL LEAVES AND BLEND TOGETHER WITH IMMERSION BLENDER.

POUR SYRUPY LIQUID THROUGH A SIEVE INTO A JUG. GET RID OF THE REMAINING PULP.

ADD JUICED LIMES INTO IT, THEN ADD CARBONATED WATER.

SERVE ON ICE, GARNISH WITH THIN ROUNDS OF LIME.

Inscribens Authorem Opery hujus
folium 266.

Frozen Butterbrew
FRAPPUCCINO

c.767.

TIME REQUIRED:
3 min

SERVINGS:
1 tall glass

Ingredients

1/3 CUP (80ML) STRONG COFFEE,
or decaf for younger wizards

1 CUP (7 LARGE CUBES) ICE

1/3 CUP (80ML) WHOLE MILK

1 TBSP SUGAR

2 TBSP BUTTERBREW SAUCE
see pancake recipe (page 6—7)

TO SERVE AS TOPPINGS: WHIPPED CREAM,
SWEET SAUCES, MINI-TREACLE FUDGE

Method

1. POUR COFFEE AND ICE CUBES
INTO A JUG BLENDER.

2. ADD MILK, SUGAR AND BUTTER-
BREW SAUCE.

Blend until smooth.

3. POUR INTO A GLASS.

4. TOP WITH WHIPPED CREAM,
DRIZZLE WITH YOUR FAVOURITE
SAUCES.

PEA Soup

Just like at the Witches' Inn

INGREDIENTS

- 1 OZ (25G) BUTTER
- 1 RED ONION, *peeled & chopped*
- 1 GARLIC CLOVE, *peeled & minced*
- 5 CUPS (750G) PEAS, *fresh or frozen*
- 1 3/4 PINTS (1 LITRE) CHICKEN STOCK
- 1/2 CUP (30G) MINT LEAVES, *torn*
- SEA SALT
- FRESHLY GROUND PEPPER, *to taste*

METHOD

In a large saucepan, slowly heat up the butter and add chopped onion. Cook on a low heat, gently stirring from time to time. After 5-7 minutes, add minced garlic and continue for another minute or two. Take care not to burn it!

Add three quarters of the peas, three quarters of stock and torn mint leaves. Cover the saucepan with a lid and cook for 10 minutes on medium heat.

Once thoroughly cooked, blend the soup with a food processor until it blends into a thick and smooth purée.

Return the purée to the saucepan, generously season with salt & pepper, then add the remaining stock and peas. Cook for another 5 minutes, then check if the newly added peas are cooked. If so, the soup is ready!

Serve immediately with a piece of crusty baguette on the side.

YORKSHIRE

PUDDING

Ingredients

- ✳ 1 1/4 CUP (150 G) PLAIN FLOUR
- ✳ 4 EGGS
- ✳ 1 CUP (200 ML) MILK
- ✳ CANOLA OIL, *for greasing*
- ✳ PINCH OF SALT
- ✳ FRESHLY GROUND PEPPER, *to taste*

Method

Preheat oven to 450°F (230°C). Brush a muffin tin with a tiny bit of canola oil and place it in the oven.

Place flour in large bowl, add in 4 eggs and beat until batter becomes smooth. Continue, slowly pouring in milk. Season well.

Take muffin tin out of the oven. Warning! It will be very hot, do be careful. Grab a ladle and pour the batter evenly into each hole. Bake for 25 minutes until puffy and golden. Serve straight away or cool down & freeze for later.

Time required:
30 min
Servings: 12

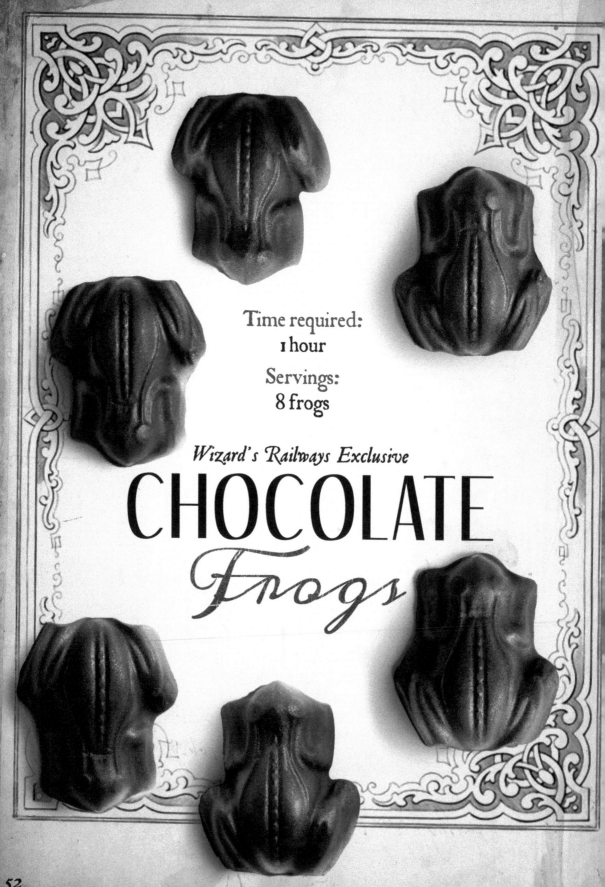

Time required:
1 hour

Servings:
8 frogs

Wizard's Railways Exclusive

CHOCOLATE
Frogs

INGREDIENTS

1 bag (11.5 oz, 326 grams) Chocolate Chips/Morsels

1/2 cup Whipped Peanut Butter

Chopped nuts of your choice (optional)

METHOD

Watch out. so they don't hop away!!!

1. Place the chocolate chips into a medium bowl. Make sure the dish is microwave safe. Microwave at 70% power for 1 minute, then stir well. Careful! The bowl gets hot.

2. Put the chocolate back into the microwave for an additional 15 seconds (again - at 70% power). Stir until chocolate has completely melted.

3. Pour about 1 tablespoon of melted chocolate into each mold. Using a silicone brush, spread the chocolate to cover the whole bottom of the mold. If you need more chocolate - add it. Freeze for 10 minutes.

4. Take the mold out of the freezer. Fill each frog with a large teaspoon of peanut butter. If you would like to stick a nut in the middle - go for it! Smooth with a spoon or a knife.

5. Pour the remaining chocolate over the peanut butter and spread it to cover each frog. Freeze again, this time for 30 minutes.

6. Pop out of the mold. Make sure they don't hop away!

WIZARDING TREAT

CAULDRON CAKES

Time required
40 minutes

Servings
12

INGREDIENTS

★ 1/2 cup (1 sticks, 112 g) Butter, softened
★ 10 tbsp (125 g) Soft Light Brown Sugar
★ 2 Large Eggs
★ 1 cup (125 g) Plain Flour
★ 3 tbsp Cocoa Powder
★ 2 tsp Baking Powder

FILLING:

★ 1 can Green Frosting/ Icing
★ Chocolate Sprinkles
(optional)

METHOD

Preheat oven to 400°F (200°C).
Grease the muffin tin or line it
with paper cases.

In a bowl, place butter, sugar and eggs.
Sift in the flour, cocoa and baking powder.
Using an electric mixer (whisking setting),
blend all ingredients together at a low speed.

Divide well-mixed batter between muffin cases.
Bake for 25 minutes. Remove to cool completely
before decorating.

Push a small circular cutter into the cupcake's
top. Carefully pop out the circle with a knife to
create a round hole. Repeat for each cupcake.

Fill each hole with a swirl of green icing.
Top with chocolate sprinkles.

Troll Fingers

MAGICAL creatures known as "Trolls" are exceptionally difficult to control and incredibly violent.

It might come as a surprise, but troll fingers are in fact a rare delicacy among connoisseurs of enchanted foods. So go on! Give them a try!

Time required:
1 h 20 min
Servings:
10-15 fingers

Yum!

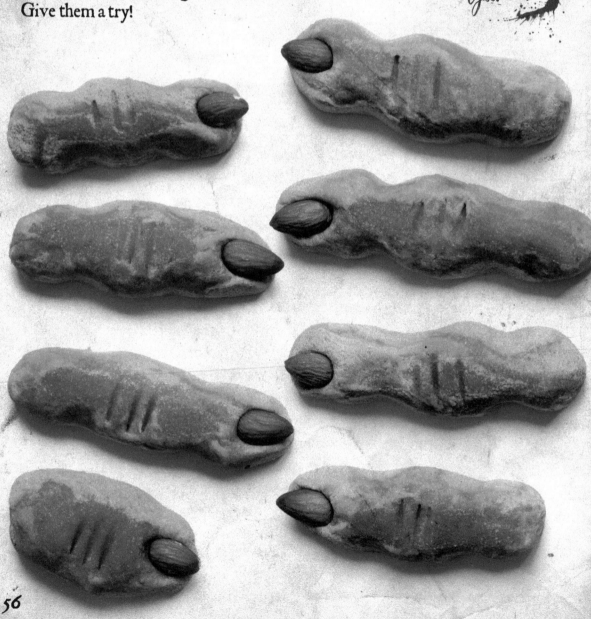

Ingredients

1 Egg · 8 oz *200 g* Butter · 1 cup *125 g* Powdered Sugar ·
1 teaspoon Almond Extract · 3 cups *350 g* All-purpose Flour ·
1 teaspoon Baking Powder · 1 teaspoon Salt ·
Green Food Colouring · ¾ cup *100 g* whole Blanched Almonds

Method

Will need an ice-cream scoop & a food processor.

Step 1 In a bowl, beat an egg together with softened butter, powdered sugar and the almond extract. Mix together using a food processor, until the texture becomes smooth and creamy. Add in the flour, baking powder and salt. Mix until a stiff dough forms.

Step 2 Add a few drops of green food colouring while mixing and cast: VIRIDI TROGLODYTARUM

Step 3 Wrap the dough tightly in a plastic wrap and refrigerate for half an hour. When the cooling period is over, divide the dough into uniform portions. To make this easier, you can use an ice cream scoop - one scoop per finger. Roll scoops of dough into finger shape for each cookie.

Step 4 Place a blanched almond on the tip of the finger and press it in firmly. Shape the tip of the finger around the almond. Squeeze to create knuckle shape. using a toothpick, mark several lines on each knuckle. Place the fingers on a lightly greased baking sheet.

Bake in a preheated oven (325ºF or 170ºC) and bake for 20-25 minutes or until just barely beginning to turn golden.

Rich dessert for Wizards and Witches with a Sweet Tooth

KNICKERBOCKER

Layered
Ice Cream Sundae with Strawberries

GLORY

Time required:
35 min
Servings:
2 cups

Try with
blueberries...

INGREDIENTS

14

For the homemade syrup: 8 oz (225 g) fresh strawberries,
5 tbsp (60g) sugar, 1/2 tsp lemon juice, 2 tbsp water

For the Knickerbocker: 2-4 scoops Vanilla Ice Cream

2-4 scoops Strawberry Ice Cream

3.5 oz (100 g) fresh Strawberries, washed and sliced

1 cup (240 ml) heavy whipping cream,
whipped with 5 drops Vanilla Extract

4 tbsp Strawberry syrup (can be store bought)

METHOD

Strawberry syrup:

Wash the strawberries and slice into pieces. Place them in cooking pan; add sugar, lemon juice and water. Mix over a medium heat, bring to boil. Reduce heat to low and cook for 20 minutes, stirring regularly. Set aside to chill completely.

For the Sundae:

In 2 tall glasses, add in a few sliced strawberries as the base layer. Cover them up with syrup.

Next, place roughly ¼ cup of whipped cream in each glass.

Add in a scoop or two of strawberry and vanilla ice cream.

Top it with the rest of the whipped cream and sliced strawberries.

Decorate with almond flakes, sprinkles or wafers (optional).

Classic
Treacle Tart

Pastry

One will also require a 9 inch (23cm) Tart Tin / Quiche Pan. Preferably with loose base.

8 oz (225 g) plain flour

1 large egg (beaten)

4 oz (110 g) diced butter

Filling

450 gram (1 lb / 1 can)

4 oz (110 g) breadcrumbs

golden syrup (light treacle)

2 pinches ground ginger

lemon zest & 2 Tbsp juice

whipped cream (optional)

Method

Place butter and flour in a bowl, mix them together with your hands until you get a breadcrumb-like consistency. Mix in the egg. Knead on a work surface dusted with flour.

Transfer the dough into a 9 inch (23cm) loose-bottomed tart dish. Push the dough into the bottom and sides of the plate. Prick the base with a fork. Place in the fridge for half an hour.

Preheat the oven to 375°F (190°C). Remove from the fridge, line the tart base with parchment paper. Fill with baking beans and bake. After 10 minutes remove beans & parchment and continue baking for another 10 minutes until golden. Remove to cool.

In a separate bowl mix together ingredients for the filling. Pour it into the baked pastry shell. Bake for 30 minutes.

Serve with a dash of whipped cream if you like!

Time required:
up to 2 hours

Servings: 6

Archmage
level

If there is one thing more than another which eludes the grasp of the beginner, is the art of making the acclaimed *School-keeper's Birthday Cake* (page 96). There are times when nothing so perfectly fits the requirements of a celebratory feast!

BUT FORGET NOT - with Archmage degree of skill, comes responsibility. If you're a Wizard of a young age, adult supervision will be needed to avoid accidents in the kitchen.

TIME REQUIRED: 1 h 20 min
SERVINGS: 4 large or 6-8 small

Pumpkin
PASTIES

FOR THE PASTY:

★ 1+1/4 cups (155 g) Plain Flour
★ 1 tbsp Sugar
★ Pinch of Salt
★ 1/2 cup (125 g) Butter, softened
★ 2 tbsp (30 ml) Ice water

Tastes better with a spell
KUKURBO COQUITO

Repeat six times
when baking.

Mix flour with sugar and salt. Cut in butter, until mixture turns into crumbs. Gradually add water, knead on a work surface dusted with flour. Form a ball and wrap it in cling-film. Place in the fridge for half an hour.

FOR THE FILLING:

- ★ 1 cup (225 g) Pumpkin Purée
- ★ 1/3 cup (75 g) Sugar
- ★ 1/4 tsp Ground Ginger and 1/2 tsp Cinnamon
- ★ 1/4 tsp Salt
- ★ 2 large Eggs

Preheat the oven to 400°F (200°C).

Place purée, sugar, spices and salt in a saucepan. Cook over a medium heat for 5 minutes, stirring from time to time. Beat eggs with a fork, set aside.

Take a dough ball out of the fridge, roll it out. Cut out circles - size is up to you. Place spoonful of filling inside each pastry circle. Brush the edge with beaten egg, then fold pastry over filling. Seal and decorate edges with a fork.

Line baking tray with parchment and transfer all pasties onto it. Using a knife, carefully make a few holes in the top. Brush all over with the egg, sprinkle with sugar. Bake for 30 minutes until golden. Serve warm or cold.

Plej bona recepto iam...

Time required: 30 min
Servings: 4 portions

Champion's

Magic Pie

Ingredients

- 4 large Potatoes
- 2 large Carrots
- 1 Onion, *chopped*
- 2 Garlic Cloves, *sliced*
- 16 oz (450 g) Ground Beef
- 2 cups (500 ml) Gravy
- 1 cup Green Beans, *canned*
- Salt and Pepper
- Olive oil
- 1 tbsp Butter

Method

Peel potatoes and carrots, slice them into chunks. Bring the water to a boil, let the potatoes cook for 10 minutes, then add carrots and cook for another 10 minutes (or until soft).

In a large frying pan, heat a few drops of olive oil, fry onion and garlic until they turn golden.

Add ground beef and fry until brown. Pour in gravy, simmer for 20 minutes. If there is too little liquid, just add some water, or better yet - some broth. Add beans and sliced carrots, season to taste.

Preheat the oven to 350°F (180°C). Move everything into a baking dish. Mash potatoes with a bit of butter, season them and use as a topping for the dish. Drizzle with olive oil and bake until golden (25 minutes or so).

TIME REQUIRED:

1 h 35 min

SERVINGS:

4–5

DRAGON
~HUNTER'S~
stew

27. Tab.

74, 1579

Ingredients

1 LBS (16 OZ, 450 G)
BRAISING BEEF

1 ONION

2 GARLIC CLOVES

4 CARROTS (10 OZ, 300 G)

FRESH PARSLEY, FRESH THYME

2 CUPS (450 ML) BEEF BROTH
(homemade or store bought)

3 TBSP TOMATO CONCENTRATE

1 TBSP RED VINEGAR

2 TBSP GRAVY GRANULES

Method

1. Preheat the oven to 350°F (180°C). Cut beef into chunks. Chop onion, garlic and carrots.

2. Take a casserole dish and add all the ingredients (leave some parsley aside for garnish). Stir to combine.

3. Bake for 90 minutes until the meat gets tender. Serve sprinkled with parsley.

FISH

& Wedges

Time required:
40 min

Servings:
4

INGREDIENTS

Fish

- 4 Fish Fillets, 6 oz (170 g) each
  Cod, Pollock, or Haddock
- Pinch of Salt
- Freshly Ground Pepper
- 1/4 cup (30 g) Plain Flour
- 1 Egg
- 1 cup (125 g) Breadcrumbs
- Canola Oil
- 1 tsp Lemon Juice

Wedges

- 4-5 Large Potatoes
- 2 tsp Olive Oil
- 1 tsp Salt
- 1/2 tsp Pepper
- 1/2 tsp Rosemary (dried)

METHOD

1. Preheat oven to 400°F (200°C).

2. Wash the potatoes - no need to peel them. Cut each potato in half lengthwise. Slice each half into four slices.

3. In a large bowl combine potatoes with olive oil, salt, pepper and rosemary. Place wedges on a baking sheet (skin side down).

4. Bake for 30-35 minutes until browned and crispy. While waiting, prepare fish fillets, as per the steps below.

5. Prepare three soup plates - one for flour, another for beaten egg, and the third for breadcrumbs.

6. Dry fish fillets with paper towel. Season with salt and pepper. Coat the fillet in flour, shake off the excess. Dip the fish in egg and then turn several times in breadcrumbs.

7. Place a large frying pan on medium-high heat, cover with roughly ½ inch (1 cm) of oil. Wait until the oil is hot before adding the fish. Add the fish to the pan and fry for about 2-4 minutes per side (until the crust gets golden).

8. Serve immediately with a squeeze of lemon.

Steak Kidney Pie

Time required:
3 hours

Servings:
4-6

You can replace the kidneys — the recipe still works!

FOR ULTIMATE WIZARDING

POWER

Ingredients

12 OZ (340 G) BRAISING STEAK

5.5 OZ (150 G) KIDNEY

2 TBSP CANOLA OIL

1 ONION, *chopped*

2 CLOVES GARLIC, *chopped*

7 OZ (200G) MUSHROOMS, *sliced*

1 1/4 CUP (300 ML) BEEF BROTH

PINCH OF SALT

FRESHLY GROUND PEPPER

CANOLA OIL

MILK, *for glazing*

Method

Chop steak & kidney meat into small chunks, season well. In a large frying pan, heat a few drops of canola oil. Brown the beef all over. Remove and set aside. In the same pan brown the kidneys. Add onions, garlic and mushrooms to the pan and fry until soft and golden. Return the steak to the pan. Pour in the broth, bring to boil. Reduce the heat down to low and simmer for 90 minutes. When meat becomes tender, pour into a large pie dish or 4-6 smaller ones. Leave to cool.

Preheat the oven to 400°F (200°C). Unfold the puff pastry sheet onto a work surface dusted with flour. Cut out circle(s), 1 inch (2.5cm) larger than your dish. Cover dish with pastry, tuck in the edges. Brush gently all over with milk and bake for 30-35 minutes, until golden.

DRAGON FLAMED ROAST

Recipe by
PROFESSOR TRIMBLE

PERFECT
DINNER

Servings: 4-5

TIME REQUIRED: 130MIN

INGREDIENTS

1 Whole Chicken *5 lbs 2.2kg*

3 tbsp Butter, *softened*

1 tsp Basil, *dried*

1 tsp Rosemary, *dried*

3 cloves Garlic, *minced*

1 tsp Fresh Parsley, *chopped*

Pinch of Salt

Freshly Ground Pepper, *to taste*

METHOD

S T E P 1

Preheat the oven to 350°F (175°C).

In a small bowl mix butter with basil, rosemary, parsley and garlic. If the mixture appears too thick, top it up with a teaspoon of olive oil.

S T E P 2

Spread the mixture all over the bird with your hands. Gently lift the skin and rub the meat underneath as well. Season with salt and pepper.

S T E P 3

Place chicken in a large baking tray. Roast for 20 minutes per pound (40 minutes per kilo), plus an additional 15 minutes.
In our case (5 lbs) it will be just under 2 hours.

You'll know it's ready when a meat thermometer inserted into the inner thigh reads at minimum of 165°F (74°C).

My favourite!

To ensure a victory in making these delicious treats, one may need special magical equipment called: "cream horn moulds".

A resourceful wizard can form moulds oneself, shaping them by hand, out of aluminium foil.

Unicorn Horns

Time required
30 min

Servings
8-12

Step 6 CAREFULLY REMOVE EACH STRAW FROM THE JAR AND RUN UNDER HOT WATER FOR A FEW MOMENTS.

Step 7 PINCH A STRAW FROM ONE END TO GRADUALLY SQUEEZE THE WORM OUT.

REPEAT WITH EACH STRAW.

SERVE IMMEDIATELY OR STORE IN A FRIDGE FOR UP TO 2 DAYS.

TOO TASTY TO RESIST

ENCHANTED CUPCAKES

Cupcakes:

- 6 tbsp (45 g) Cocoa Powder
- 4 tbsp Water *boiling*
- 3 medium Eggs
- 3/4 cup (190 g) Butter, *softened*
- 1 cup (170 g) Light Brown Sugar
- 1 cup (125 g) Self-raising Flour
- 1 tsp Baking Powder

Frosting:

- 1 cup (7 oz, 200 g) Butterscotch Flavoured Morsels
- 3 tbsp Whipping Cream
- 1/2 cup (1 stick, 112g) Butter
- 1 tsp Butter Extract
- Pinch of Salt
- 3 cups (375 g) Icing Sugar
- 1/4 cup (2 oz, 60 ml) Cream Soda

INGREDIENTS

For the Cupcakes:

1. Preheat oven to 400°F (200°C). Grease muffin tin or line it with paper cases.

2. Prepare a medium bowl. Sift in the cocoa powder, add boiling water. Mix together with a fork into a chocolatey paste. Add the rest of the ingredients. Using an electric mixer (whisking setting) blend all ingredients together at a low speed.

3. Divide batter equally between the muffin cases. Bake for 15 minutes until well risen. Remove to cool completely before decorating.

Butter Ale Frosting:

- Place morsels, cream and salt in a microwave-safe bowl. Set the microwave onto a medium setting for 60 seconds. Stir carefully (warning: the bowl can get hot!).

If the consistency is still too thick, microwave for another 15 seconds and repeat if necessary. Set aside to cool.

- In a large mixing bowl whip the butter until fluffy. Spoon in the butterscotch mixture, then add butter extract. Mix until combined. Slowly add the sugar 1 cup at a time alternating with the cream soda.

If frosting becomes too thin, add more icing sugar. Beat until smooth and fluffy.

- Fill a piping bag with frosting. Pipe swirls of thick, rich frosting onto cupcakes. Decorate with sprinkles.

Bon Appétit!

When they say...

they mean it!

Jelly Beans

Time Required
40 MINUTES
+ OVERNIGHT
+ 2 DAYS

Servings
A LOT

Ingredients

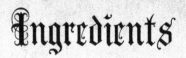

3 TBSP UNFLAVOURED GELATIN
(AROUND 4 ENVELOPES)

3/4 CUPS (175 ML) COLD WATER

1 CUP (235 ML) BOILING WATER

3 CUPS (600 G) FINE SUGAR,
PLUS EXTRA FOR COATING

CHOSEN FLAVOUR EXTRACTS:
CITRUS, STRAWBERRY,
COCONUT...

CHOSEN FOOD COLOURINGS

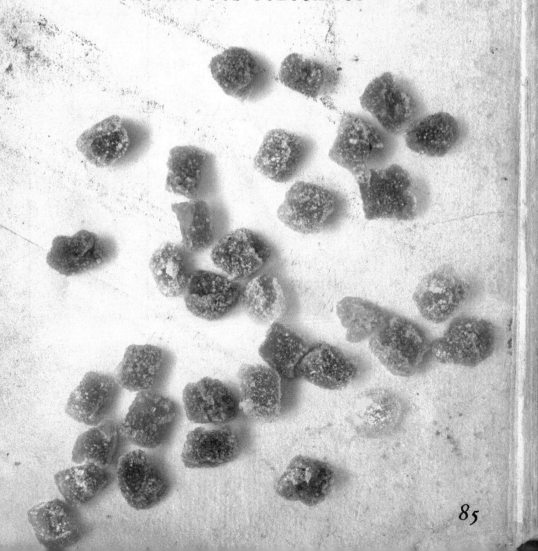

Method

Step 1

LINE A NUMBER OF SMALL RECTANGULAR CONTAINERS WITH CLING FILM. SET ASIDE.

Step 2

POUR COLD WATER INTO A LARGE COOKING POT. SPRINKLE GELATIN, STIR AND LET IT REST FOR 5 MINUTES.

Step 3

ADD BOILING WATER AND STIR FOR THE GELATIN TO DISSOLVE. MIX IN SUGAR. COOK ON A HIGH HEAT, STIRRING CONSTANTLY UNTIL THE MIXTURE BOILS.

REDUCE HEAT AND LET THE MIXTURE SIMMER FOR 20-25 MINUTES, STIRRING CONSTANTLY. REMOVE FROM HEAT.

Step 4

PREPARE A COUPLE OF BOWLS (DEPENDING ON NUMBER OF COLOURS & FLAVOURS YOU'RE AIMING FOR).

CAREFULLY POUR SOME OF THE MIXTURE TO EACH ONE. ADD 2-3 DROPS OF COLOURING/EXTRACTS TO EACH BOWL AND STIR WELL.

Step 5

SPRAY RECTANGULAR CONTAINERS WITH NON-STICK SPRAY. POUR THE MIXTURES INTO EACH ONE. COVER WITH PLASTIC AND LET THEM COOL.

Step 6

WHEN COOLED, TRANSFER TO REFRIGERATOR AND CHILL OVERNIGHT. THE NEXT DAY, SPRINKLE CUTTING BOARD WITH SUGAR. PEEL OFF HARDENED CANDY FROM CONTAINERS.

GREASE A KNIFE WITH SOME OIL OR BUTTER AND CUT CANDY INTO SMALL BEANS. COAT EACH BEAN WITH SUGAR.

Step 7

LEAVE THE SWEETS OUT ON PARCHMENT AT ROOM TEMPERATURE FOR A DAY. WITH TIME, SUGAR WILL CRYSTALLIZE, CREATING A HARD SHELL.
STORE IN A JAR.

TIME REQUIRED:
30 MINUTES

SERVINGS:
A LOT!

Lemon

SHERBETS

Wizarding Classic

INGREDIENTS

* 1 CUP (200 G) SUGAR
* 1/4 CUP (3 OZ, 85 G) HONEY
* 3-4 TBSP WATER
* 2 TSP CITRIC ACID
* 3-4 DROPS YELLOW FOOD COLOURING
* CITRUS FLAVOURING
* SUPERFINE/CASTER SUGAR FOR DUSTING

   YOU'LL ALSO NEED: CANDY THERMOMETER, KITCHEN SCISSORS

METHOD

LINE A SMALL BAKING TRAY WITH PARCHMENT PAPER.

POUR IN SUGAR, HONEY, AND WATER INTO A LARGE POT. COOK ON A HIGH HEAT, STIRRING CONSTANTLY UNTIL THE MIXTURE BOILS.

DO NOT STIR ANYMORE AT THIS POINT, WAIT UNTIL IT REACHES 310°F (150°C). TURN OFF THE HEAT. SET ASIDE FOR A MINUTE.

POUR IN A FEW DROPS OF COLOURING AND FLAVOURING. ADD CITRIC ACID AND STIR WELL. POUR THE MIXTURE INTO PARCHMENT-LINED PAN. WAIT UNTIL IT HARDENS A BIT (AROUND 5 MINUTES).

USING KNIFE OR KITCHEN SCISSORS CUT OUT THE IN-DIVIDUAL SHERBETS. DUST WITH SUGAR TO KEEP THE CANDY FROM STICKING TOGETHER. LEAVE TO COOL. STORE IN A DARK, COOL PLACE.

LIQUORICE WANDS

TIME REQUIRED:
1 hour

SERVINGS:
10-12 wands

INGREDIENTS

1 cup (200 g) Sugar

¾ cup (255 g) Maple Syrup

½ cup (1 stick, 112g) Butter

½ cup (150g) Sweetened
Condensed Milk

¾ cup (100 g) Bread Flour

2 tbsp Anise Extract

Pinch of Salt

Brown Food Colouring

Spell:
SUAVIS
when twisting
the wands

METHOD

Pour in sugar, syrup, butter, milk and salt into a large pot.
Cook at a high heat, stirring constantly until the mixture reaches
260°F (125°C). Turn off the heat. Whisk in flour, anise extract
and food colouring until the texture becomes smooth.

Line a square tray (8x8 inch /20x20cm) with parchment paper
and pour in the mixture. Spread it out with a spoon or spatula.
Cool for 30 min in the fridge.

Remove from tray. With a sharp knife, cut elongated triangles.
Starting with the widest point, twist the wand at the base.
Continue until the wand is shaped. Repeat with the rest of the
candy triangles. Cool for another 5 minutes to make them keep
their shape.

TIME REQUIRED:
20 MIN + OVERNIGHT

SERVINGS:
6-8

BUTTERALE
Ice Cream

INGREDIENTS

* 3/4 CUP (150 G) PURE DARK CANE SUGAR
* 14 OZ (400 G; 1 CAN) EVAPORATED MILK
* 3/4 CUP (180 ML) DOUBLE / HEAVY CREAM
* 1 EGG WHITE
* TREACLE FUDGE PIECES (TO DECORATE)
* WAFFLE CONES (OPTIONAL)

METHOD

PLACE SUGAR IN A LARGE BOWL, POUR THE MILK IN. USING ELECTRIC MIXER (WHISKING SETTING) BLEND THE INGREDIENTS TOGETHER UNTIL THE MIXTURE THICKENS.

IN ANOTHER BOWL, WHISK CREAM UNTIL IT THICKENS (BUT IS NOT STIFFENING YET).

GET A THIRD BOWL, WASH THE BEATERS AND WHISK THE EGG WHITE UNTIL IT GETS STIFF GENTLY FOLD THE CREAM INTO THE SUGARY MIXTURE WITH A SPATULA. ADD IN THE EGG WHITE. SLOWLY COMBINE TOGETHER WITH A SPATULA.

POUR ICE CREAM INTO A PLASTIC CONTAINER, COVER AND PLACE IN THE FREEZER OVERNIGHT.

IF ICE CREAM GETS TOO SOLID, REMOVE FROM THE FREEZER AND PLACE IN THE REFRIGERATOR FOR A FEW MINUTES BEFORE SERVING.

DECORATE WITH SMALL TREACLE FUDGE PIECES

CANARY

Time required:
up to 4 hours

Servings:
6-8

CREAM PIE

INGREDIENTS

2 Egg Yolks *(keep egg whites for the filling)* · 1/2 cup *(1 stick, 112 g)* Butter
1/2 cup *(125 g)* Icing / Powdered Sugar ·
2 cups *(250 g)* Plain Flour, *plus extra for dusting* · A pinch of Salt

FOR THE FILLING: 3 Lemons, *zested and juiced:* 2/3 cup juice *(150 ml)* ·
1/2 cup *(100 g)* Fine / Caster sugar · 4 Eggs ·
3/4 cup *(180 ml)* Heavy Cream · 1 tbsp Icing / Powdered Sugar
for dusting

METHOD

STEP 1 Separate yolks from whites, set aside. Place butter and sugar in a large bowl, beat until softened. Sieve in the flour, add salt and yolks. Continue mixing until the dough becomes sticky. Shape into a ball, wrap in cling-film and rest in the fridge for 90 minutes.

STEP 2 Flour your rolling surface and rolling pin. Roll out the pastry, rotating the dough as you go. Aim for a thickness of 1/8 inch (3 mm). Transfer the dough into a 10 inch (25 cm) loose-bottomed tart dish. Push the dough into the bottom and sides of the plate. Prick the base with a fork. Trim the excess. Refrigerate for half an hour.

STEP 3 Preheat the oven to 350ºF (180ºC). Remove from the fridge, line with parchment paper. Fill with baking beans and bake. After 10 minutes remove beans & parchment and continue baking for another 10 minutes until golden. Remove to cool.

STEP 4 Reduce the temperature to 300ºF (150ºC). Prepare the filling. Place lemon juice, sugar and eggs (plus additional egg whites you kept from the base) in a bowl, whisk until smooth. Push this mix through a sieve into another bowl. Add lemon zest and cream, mix gently. Move the filling to the tart case with a spoon. Bake for 45 minutes until the filling sets.

STEP 5 Let it cool gradually - switch off the oven, open the doors and let it cool inside for a while. Once cooled, dust with icing sugar.

The Schoolkeeper's
BIRTHDAY CAKE

TIME REQUIRED:
1 hour

SERVINGS:
8

Ingredients

FOR THE SPONGE
- ✦ 1 cup (8 oz/2 US sticks/227 grams) Butter, softened
- ✦ 1 cup (7 oz/200 grams) Caster / Super fine Sugar
- ✦ 1+3/4 cup (7.7 oz/220 grams) Self-Raising Flour
- ✦ 4 Eggs
- ✦ 1 tsp Vanilla Extract
- ✦ 1 tsp Baking Powder
- ✦ 3 tbsp Cocoa Powder
- ✦ 3 tbsp Milk
- ✦ Pinch of Salt

FOR THE PINK CREAM
- ✦ 2 cups (16 oz / 450g) Mascarpone Cheese
- ✦ Pinch of Salt
- ✦ 1 cup Double Cream / Heavy Cream
- ✦ 2/3 cup Powdered Sugar
- ✦ 1 tsp Vanilla Extract
- ✦ Food Colouring: red or pink

FOR DECORATION
- ✦ 1 tube Decorating Icing / Icing Writer: in green

Method

FOR THE SPONGE

1. Preheat the oven to 350°F (180°C). Grease your cake tin (in this case we've used 3 shallow 8 inch/20cm tins; but you can use one deep one and then just slice into three layers after baking) and set aside.

2. In a large mixing bowl, place the softened butter and sugar, then beat together until pale.

3. Add the rest of the ingredients and continue beating until the mixture becomes smooth.

4. Divide the batter between each cake tin, gently smoothen the tops.

5. Bake for 25 minutes. If you're not sure whether it's ready, insert a skewer - if it comes out clean, it's done!

6. Don't remove from the tins until the sponge has cooled down a bit, 10 minutes should be enough. Remove the cake from the tins and transfer to a cooling rack.

FOR THE PINK CREAM

1. You'll need an electric mixer for this one. Place the mascarpone and salt in a large mixing bowl. Mix it together on low speed.

2. While the motor is running, pour in the cream - slowly, gradually, not all at once. Then increase the speed a bit and start beating in the sugar. Continue until you see "blobs" forming.

3. This should make around 4 cups of creamy deliciousness. Set aside two thirds of the cream - you'll need it for the cake's filling.

4. Add food colouring to the remaining 1/3 of the cream. A few drops should be enough. Use the mixer on medium setting and give it a good mix.

PUTTING IT ALL TOGETHER

4ᵞ.
Sz: IV.
P. 1.

1. Once the sponges are cooled, lay one with the topside down on a cake stand. Spread with half of your "white" mixture.

Top with another sponge (topside up this time) and push down gently. Spread another half of the white cream and top with the last layer of the cake.

2. Ice the top of the cake with the pink mascarpone mixture by piling it in the centre. Then spread it to the sides, then gradually bring it down the sides. Smooth with a spoon (or a palette knife if you have one).

3. Last, but not least - use a green icing marker to write "Happee birthdae" and the name of the Birthday boy or Birthday girl.

RECIPE INDEX

Breakfasts

Lunch & Dinner

Beverages

Cookies & Cakes

Desserts

Candies & Sweets

"Magical Kitchen" is available at quantity discounts for bulk purchases. For more information, send your owl to:
hello@artofwizardry.com

This edition was printed by a print-on-demand service. For an exclusive Special Edition, visit: artofwizardry.com/special-edition